❋The All-Around Christmas Book

The All-Around Christmas Book

by Margery Cuyler

illustrated by Corbett Jones

❀ ❀ ❀

Holt, Rinehart and Winston · New York

Acknowledgments

Special thanks go to my mother, who helped me
with my research; to Paula Krimsky, who provided me
with information on Christmas in Russia; and to
Juliana McIntyre and Sarah Perkins, the children
who tested the crafts.

Published by Holt, Rinehart and Winston,
383 Madison Avenue, New York, New York 10017.

Published simultaneously in Canada by Holt, Rinehart and
Winston of Canada, Limited.

Library of Congress Cataloging in Publication Data
Cuyler, Margery.   The all-around Christmas book.

Summary: Includes discussions of the origin and
symbolism of Christmas, together with Christmas-
related crafts and recipes.
1. Christmas—Juvenile literature. 2. Christmas—
Exercises, recitations, etc. [1. Christmas.
2. Handicraft. 3. Christmas cookery. 4. Cookery]
I. Jones, Corbett, ill. II. Title.
BV45.C89 1982   263′.91   82-3104   AACR2
ISBN Hardbound: 0-03-060387-0
ISBN Paperback: 0-03-062183-6

Printed in the United States of America
10   9   8   7   6   5   4

ISBN 0-03-060387-0 HARDBOUND
ISBN 0-03-062183-6 PAPERBACK

For Muriel and Jack,
with thanks for Jan

❊ Contents

1 • How Christmas Began 1

2 • The Christmas Calendar 6

3 • Greens and Plants 9

4 • Crèches, Carols, and Cards 21

5 • Christmas Eve 29

6 • Santa Claus 33

7 • Christmas Around the World 38

8 • Christmas in the Kitchen 49

9 • Christmas Crafts 67

10 • Christmas Games 84

List of Suggested Reading 87

Index 88

1 ❋ How Christmas Began

❋ ❋ ❋ Christmas, the Christian holiday that celebrates the birth of Christ, takes place on December 25.

It is an exciting, happy day when family and friends gather together to exchange gifts and share a festive meal. At the beginning of December, people start wrapping presents, hanging wreaths and mistletoe, decorating evergreen trees with ornaments, and sending pretty cards to old friends. The kitchen is filled with the smells of cakes and breads being baked for a big meal on Christmas Day. Party dishes are taken out of storage, and Christmas music is heard everywhere. On Christmas Eve, children leave a snack for Santa Claus and his reindeer, and in some houses and towns, adults light a yule log. When the great day arrives, people flock to church to hear the story of Christ's birth read aloud, to pray, and to sing hymns and carols.

The story of the birth of Christ is in the part of the Bible called the New Testament. There it is written that before Christ was born, God sent an angel to Mary, a young woman who was getting ready to marry a carpenter named Joseph. The angel said: "And behold, thou shalt conceive in thy womb, and bring forth a son, and shalt call His name Jesus. He shall be great, and shall be called the son of the Highest."

Because Mary believed in God, she believed the angel. She knew that God had picked her to be the mother of his son. She had the baby in Bethlehem and named him Jesus, just as the angel had told her to do. He was born in a stable because Mary and Joseph were unable to find room in an inn.

On the night Jesus was born, another angel appeared to shepherds in a field and said: "Fear not, for behold, I bring you good tidings of great joy, which shall be to all people. For unto you is born this day in the city of David a Saviour, which is Christ the Lord. And this shall be a sign unto you. Ye shall find the babe wrapped in swaddling clothes, lying in a manger."

The shepherds hurried to Bethlehem and found Mary, Joseph, and Jesus in the stable. The shepherds believed that Jesus was the son of God and left to tell everyone what they had seen.

On the same night, three Magi—men from Persia who studied the stars as part of their religion—saw a bright star in the East. They followed it to Bethlehem, where they found Christ lying in a manger. When they saw the baby, they gave him gifts and worshiped him.

Today, the Magi are also called "the three kings." But this term was not used widely until more than five hundred years after Christ's death.

Even though Christmas is celebrated on December 25, that date is not Christ's real birthday. No one knows the exact date of his birth. Many scholars believe that, before the fourth century, his birthday was honored on January 6 and called the Nativity. Also on that date, a festival, Epiphany, was held to celebrate Christ's baptism and the Magi's visit to the stable

in Bethlehem. It wasn't until A.D. 353 that Pope Liberius in Rome declared December 25 a Christian holiday to mark the birth of Christ.

At that time, Rome was the center of the world. Roman armies had conquered many countries, including what are now the British Isles, Northern Africa, Spain, and the Middle East. Because the Romans ruled all these countries, the empire was made up of many different cultures and religions. Only a tenth of the people in the empire were Christian. The other nine-tenths were called "pagans" by the Christians.

They celebrated their own festivals on or near December 25. Perhaps Pope Liberius moved the Nativity holiday up to December 25 so that Christians would not be tempted to join in the pagan festivals that occurred at the same time.

One of the most popular pagan festivals, Saturnalia, took place from December 17 until December 24. Since the fall crops were planted and autumn was drawing to a close, it was held in honor of Saturnus, the god of the harvest. Men and women, holding lighted candles, paraded through the streets in masks and costumes. Schools were closed, and people were allowed to gamble, which at other times of the year was against the law. Masters and slaves switched roles. The slaves picked a slave-king, "The Lord of Misrule," who ordered everyone, including the rich, to wait on him and perform games and tricks. The rich and poor gave each other gifts like candles, dolls, and holly branches. Everywhere, the pagans stopped work to celebrate this favorite holiday. Christians must have wanted to join the fun until the Pope gave them their own holiday.

Another pagan festival, *Natalis Solis Invicti,* fell on December 25. It was a feast for the "birth of the unconquered sun." It became very popular among the Roman soldiers when they conquered Persia in the middle of the first century. Mithras, a Persian sun god, was said to have slain a bull from which all life began. Mithras stood for goodness, justice and life everlasting. The Roman soldiers prayed to him to help them win battles. A feast in his honor was held on December 25 because it was the winter solstice—the time of year when days grew longer. People in ancient times believed this meant the sun was conquering darkness, just as Mithras had conquered the bull.

Besides Saturnalia and *Natalis Solis Invicti,* there was a pagan holiday called Kalends. It was a New Year's celebration that began on January 1 and lasted three days. The Romans decorated their houses with lights and plants. They gave special gifts to friends, children, and the poor. They believed that gifts of gold and silver brought wealth, lamps brought warmth, and honey brought luck. The Romans saved their money all year so they could spend it having a good time during Kalends.

Many of our most beautiful Christmas customs come from these ancient festivals.

2 ✸ The Christmas Calendar

✸ ✸ ✸ After December 25 was picked as the Christmas holiday, the month before was set aside as a season of fasting and prayer. It was called Advent, which comes from the Latin word meaning "to come." People used this time to prepare for Christ's coming into the world. Advent starts on the fourth Sunday before Christmas and ends on Christmas Day. It is still observed by many Christians.

Christians celebrate Advent by going to church on the four Sundays before Christmas. They also hang Advent wreaths in their homes and churches. The round shape goes back to the Saturnalia festival, when people stopped work and hung up their wagon wheels. They decorated them with evergreens and lighted candles. The flames stood for the light brought

into the world by the return of the sun. Like the pagans, Christians today light candles during the Christmas season. On each Sunday before Christmas, they light one candle and place it on their Advent wreath. Because this is a fire hazard, some families use electric candles. Others place the candles on a nearby table or window. Then, on Christmas Eve, a large candle is lit to honor Christ. This light stands for the light he brought into the world when he was born.

There are also nine days before Christmas—the *posadas* days—that are celebrated by Spanish-speaking Americans. *Posada* is the Spanish word for inn. During these nine days, people act out Mary and Joseph's search for the inn in Bethlehem. The manger for the baby Jesus is left empty until Christmas Day, when a doll is added to stand for Christ.

Christmas is celebrated on January 7 by many Greek and Russian Orthodox churches. On the Gregorian calendar which they follow, January 7 is the same as December 25.

Even though many people celebrate Christmas for only one day, Christmas actually lasts for twelve days. These twelve days begin on Christmas Eve and last until Epiphany on January 6. As mentioned in Chapter 1, Epiphany was an early Roman festival that honored the Magi's visit to Bethlehem. Today, Epiphany mainly marks the end of the Christmas season. It is a time to take down decorations in homes and churches. Only in a very few churches do decorations stay up until February 2, the Festival of Candlemas. In some churches this is the day on which candles are blessed for the coming year.

❀ Christmas Calendar

The fourth Sunday before Christmas
> First day of Advent

December 6
> St. Nicholas's Day

December 13
> St. Lucia's Day

December 16–25
> *Posadas* days

December 24
> Christmas Eve

December 25
> Christmas Day

December 26
> Boxing Day

January 5
> Epiphany Eve

January 6
> Epiphany

January 7
> Greek and Russian Orthodox Christmas

January 13
> St. Knut's Day

February 2
> Candlemas

3 ✻ Greens and Plants

✻ ✻ ✻ At Christmas, people bring beautiful outdoor greens inside to decorate their homes. They hang garlands—strings of evergreen branches—around window and door frames. They wrap them around banisters and lay them across mantelpieces. They make lovely wreaths out of holly and ivy and hang mistletoe from the ceiling. They attach ornaments, lights, and tinsel to an evergreen tree that has been brought indoors. And they fill their houses with flowering plants especially grown for Christmas.

Using plants and greens as winter decorations began more than two thousand years ago—before the time when Christ was born.

Evergreens

Evergreens are plants and trees, such as holly, laurel, and pine, that stay green all year round. They are "ever green"

during winter, when the other trees have lost their leaves. The pagans believed that evergreens stood for life. When the sun was at its lowest point in the sky, the pagans brought evergreens inside, believing this would help the sun rise again. They also used evergreens to scare off the ghosts and witches they thought had crept into their homes to get warm. They hung holly leaves to prick witches and burned juniper berries to chase away demons.

Evergreens with berries—mistletoe, holly, and ivy—were considered sacred.

Mistletoe

About twenty-two hundred years ago, a group of people called the Celts lived in what are now the British Isles and France. Their priests, or Druids, killed animals and people as gifts to the gods. They wanted the gods to protect them from evil spirits and witches. The Druids believed that the mistletoe which grew on oak trees had special powers. They thought that during winter the oak tree god lived in the mistletoe after the oak branches died. When the winter solstice came, the high priest, dressed in white, climbed an oak tree and cut down the mistletoe with a golden sickle. The mistletoe was caught by a white cloth, so that it wouldn't touch the ground where the witches could harm it. Then the Druids placed part of the mistletoe on an altar and killed two white bulls as a gift to the gods. Afterward, they divided the rest of the mistletoe and gave it to the townspeople to hang over their doors for good luck. The Druids called the mistletoe "all healer." They thought that if childless women and animals

ate it, they would be able to have babies. They believed that it cured epilepsy. Because it grew high up and didn't touch the ground, epileptics ate it to keep from falling down. It was also supposed to heal skin ulcers and protect people from being poisoned.

Today, people kiss each other under mistletoe. This custom comes from a Scandinavian legend: An ancient god named Balder had a dream that he was going to die. He was so worried that he shared his dream with his mother, the goddess Frigga. She became alarmed and in an effort to protect her son, she made everyone and everything promise not to harm him. But she forgot to ask the mistletoe, since she didn't think the plant was important enough to cause any trouble. There was another god named Loki who was very jealous of Balder.

When he found out that Frigga had ignored the mistletoe, he asked the blind god Hother to hurl a mistletoe dart at Balder. Hother did as Loki asked, and the dart pierced Balder and killed him. Frigga was very sad to have lost her son. She cried so much that her tears became the white berries on the mistletoe plant. Frigga pleaded with the gods to bring Balder back to life. Since they too loved Balder, they agreed to do so. Frigga was happy again. She stood under the mistletoe's white berries and kissed everyone who passed beneath. In time, mistletoe became a symbol of peace and love. If enemies met below it, they laid down their arms and made peace.

Because of its pagan origins, mistletoe is not usually allowed inside churches. But it is hung in homes, where people kiss under it to heal pain, end arguments, and bring good luck.

Holly and Ivy

The leaders of the early Church wanted to get rid of the pagan custom of bringing evergreens indoors. But the pagans kept doing so, even after some of them became Christians. So finally the leaders decided to make evergreens part of the story of Christ's life. A legend began that the crown of thorns Christ wore before his death was made of holly leaves. When the crown pricked Christ's forehead, his blood flowed over the holly berries, changing them from white to red.

The early English carol below shows that holly had become part of the Christmas story by the sixteenth century:

The Holly and the Ivy

Holly

The holly and the ivy,
When they are both full grown,
Of all the trees that are in the wood,
The holly bears the crown:
 The rising of the sun
 And the running of the deer,
 The playing of the merry organ,
 Sweet singing in the choir.

Ivy

The holly bears a blossom,
As white as lily flower,
And Mary bore sweet Jesus Christ
To do poor sinners good.
 Chorus

The holly bears a prickle,
As sharp as any thorn,
And Mary bore sweet Jesus Christ
On Christmas Day in the morn.
 Chorus

The holly bears a bark,
As bitter as any gall,
And Mary bore sweet Jesus Christ
For to redeem us all.
   Chorus

After the early Church accepted holly, it was used as a Christmas decoration.

Ivy, on the other hand, took a much longer time to be accepted because ivy was the symbol of an ancient Roman god named Bacchus. He was the god of wine and could make people happy or miserable, depending upon how much wine they drank. The Church didn't approve of people getting drunk. As a result, the symbol for the god of wine was not brought into the early Church. As time passed, however, ivy became a symbol for everlasting life, and was used as a Christmas decoration also.

In most early English carols, holly and ivy were mentioned together since they were symbols for the male and female halves of human nature. Holly became known as a "man's plant" because it protected itself with thorns in the same way a man would protect himself with weapons. Ivy was known as a "woman's plant" because it had to be supported by a wall or tree in the same way women were thought to need the support of men in the Middle Ages.

Rosemary

There are two things that are special about rosemary—its sweet aroma and its beautiful gray-green color. According to a

legend, it received its smell when Mary hung Jesus's baby blankets over it. It received its color from her cloak, which she threw on its branches. In the Middle Ages, people spread rosemary on floors so their houses would smell good. By the nineteenth century, it was used in England to flavor the boar's head that was cooked for the Christmas feast. Now, it's used mainly as a food seasoning.

The Christmas Tree

Our modern Christmas tree stands for life, as evergreens did before Christ was born. But the custom of cutting down a whole tree and bringing it indoors is just a few hundred years old. As far as anyone knows, only branches were brought indoors during the pagan festivals. And to this day, it's unclear how the custom of decorating Christmas trees began.

Some people think it was started in Germany in the fifteenth century by a famous monk named Martin Luther. A popular story says that while he was walking through the woods on Christmas Eve, he looked up and saw stars sparkling through the branches of a fir tree. He was so struck by the sky's beauty that he cut down the fir tree, carried it home, and decorated it with lighted candles. He wanted to show how it had looked when it was lit up by starlight.

There are some even earlier legends about the Christmas tree. In the tenth century, a man named Georg Jacob told a story in which all the trees in the world bloomed on the night Christ was born. And there's a French legend from the thirteenth century about an enormous tree lit with candles that could be seen in a forest on Christmas Eve. At the top of the tree, baby Jesus rested with a halo around his head.

These are only legends. But there is a real story about decorated evergreen branches that might explain the first Christmas trees. During the Middle Ages, German peasants performed plays in front of churches on December 25. These plays were about Adam and Eve, the first man and woman made by God. The players acted out the story of how God cast Adam and Eve out of the Garden of Eden after they ate an apple from the tree of good and evil. The players hung apples on an evergreen branch to stand for the tree.

When the Church leaders no longer allowed these plays to be performed, people started to bring "Adam and Eve trees" into their homes on December 25. They brought both evergreen branches and small fir trees indoors. They decorated them with apples, and with roses and wafers to stand for Mary and Christ. They called these decorated evergreens *Christbaum*. They often placed Christbaum next to two other Christmas shapes. One was called a *pyramid*, a wooden frame that held branches and candles. The other was called a *lichtstock*, a flat triangle that held candles. Perhaps people thought candles would look nice on the Christbaum when they saw it next to the lichtstock and pyramid. Whatever the reason, by the 1700s, Germans were decorating small indoor trees with candles.

Christbaum   *Pyramid*   *Lichtstock*

In the nineteenth century, Christmas trees became popular in England. This was because Queen Victoria's German husband, Albert, missed Christmas trees when he married and moved to England. So in 1841 he started the custom of decorating a large tree in Windsor Castle. Soon everyone in England was decorating Christmas trees.

Germans also brought the Christmas tree to America. As

early as 1747, trees were being decorated in Bethlehem, Pennsylvania, by a group of Germans called Moravians. Christmas
trees didn't become really popular in America, however, until
the twentieth century. That's when it became possible to trim
trees with electric lights and handmade glass ornaments. So
many trees were being cut down that one year President The-
odore Roosevelt banned the Christmas tree from the White
House. (Even so, his sons Archie and Quentin smuggled a
Christmas tree into Archie's closet!) Today, trees are grown on
special farms just for Christmas. They're much taller and
larger than the tiny fir trees first used at Christmas in the
Middle Ages.

18

Trimming the Tree

The Germans in the Middle Ages decorated their fir trees with nuts, fruits, gingerbread, paper roses, candies, and home-made paper ornaments. Their trees became especially beautiful when they began to attach candles to the branches. Since candles were a fire hazard, it was a great relief when Thomas Alva Edison invented the electric light bulb in 1879. One of his best friends, Edward Johnson, tried using electric lights on a Christmas tree in 1882. Then, in 1895, President Grover Cleveland decorated the tree at the White House with electric lights. Finally, electric lights on strings were invented in 1907, and the invention spread rapidly across the country.

Today, people have many choices for trimming their trees. They can fill them with homemade decorations, ornaments bought in a store, or a combination of both. It's very unusual to see two trees that look alike. Decorating a tree is a wonderful way to bring people together and to do something creative at Christmas.

Poinsettia

This colorful Christmas plant is named for Joel R. Poinsett, America's first minister to Mexico. He brought it back to the United States, where it was named for him in 1836.

19

The poinsettia is prized in Mexico at Christmas because of its appearance in a popular legend. The early Mexicans flocked to church on Christmas Eve in Cuernavaca to fill Christ's manger with flowers. One year, a poor boy became heartbroken when he couldn't find any flowers to take to the church. An angel appeared to him and told him to pick some weeds from the side of the road. The boy did as the angel said, then brought the weeds to the church. When he placed them in the manger, they changed into scarlet flowers. Mexicans call the poinsettia the *Flor de la Noche Buena,* the Flower of the Holy Night.

Poinsettias are sometimes white as well as red. Most of them come from California, where they are raised especially for use as Christmas gifts and decorations. The city of Ventura, California, is even called Poinsettia City.

People celebrate Christmas with other beautiful Christmas plants besides the poinsettia. People used to bring plants indoors in the Middle Ages, hoping that they would bloom at Christmas. Early Australians named all the flowering trees they found at Christmas, Christmas Bush or Christmas Tree. In warm climates, palms, mosses, and ferns became popular Christmas plants. And the rose, which grows in Central Europe in the middle of winter, is a favorite overseas holiday plant. Today, gardeners grow hothouse plants that will bloom all through the holiday.

There's no end to the gorgeous plants and trees that add a special flavor to the Christmas season.

4 ❃ Crèches, Carols, and Cards

The Christmas Crèche

❃ ❃ ❃ One of the nicest Christmas customs is the setting up of a crèche during Advent. A crèche is a man-made scene of the night when Christ was born in the stable at Bethlehem. A tiny figure of baby Jesus is placed in an open manger or crib— a small feeding box for cows and horses. Then figures of Mary, Joseph, the three Magi, shepherds, angels, and farm animals are arranged around the manger. The crèche is set up under a Christmas tree or in some special place in the house. At church, it is displayed in a spot that can easily be seen by people walking by, or outdoors.

The word *crèche* is the French word for manger. The French word probably comes from the Italian word *Greccio*. Greccio was the town in which a famous crèche was set up by St.

Francis of Assisi in the thirteenth century. When Francis was alive, mangers were built in churches all over Italy at Christmas. Francis probably even visited the Church of Santa Maria Maggiore in Rome, where the very first manger was made in the fourth century. But many of these early church mangers were covered with gold, silver, and jewels. They were much fancier than the simple manger in which Christ was laid. Francis felt it was important for people to remember that Christ was born in a humble stable. In 1223 Francis asked a friend of his who lived in Greccio to take an ass, an ox, a manger, and some straw to a nearby cave. When this was done, Francis, the friars, and the local people met in the cave by candlelight on Christmas Eve. They acted out the story of Christ's birth. It must have been a very moving sight.

After St. Francis made the crèche popular, it appeared in homes and churches all over the world. The custom didn't come to America until 1741 when the Moravians settled in Bethlehem, Pennsylvania. They brought *putzes* or large, fancy crèches with them from Germany. Their putzes sometimes had bridges, houses, fences, gardens, waterfalls, and even fountains. Today, the German-Americans in Pennsylvania still set up these remarkable crèches at Christmas.

People from other nations also brought crèches to America. They are now an important part of our Christmas season.

Christmas Carols

The merry music of Christmas can be heard everywhere during December. People band together and walk up and down streets, singing Christmas carols beneath windows. Car-

ols are sung in church on Christmas Eve and Christmas Day, and people like to sing them at parties or listen to them on records. They're heard on TV, on the radio, in banks, in schools, and in stores all over America. Christmas is a musical time of year, and the words of "Silent Night," "We Three Kings of Orient Are," "O Little Town of Bethlehem," "Away in a Manger," and other carols bring joy to everyone's heart.

The word *carol* comes from the Greek word *choraulein,* which was an ancient dance performed in a circle to flute music. The Romans borrowed the custom from the Greeks and later brought it to England. In the Middle Ages, the English danced in a ring to singing voices. They used the word *carol* to describe what they were doing. Finally, *carol* changed from meaning a dance to meaning a song.

Besides making the crèche popular at Christmas, St. Francis of Assisi wrote beautiful Christmas hymns. The friars who followed him also wrote joyous hymns. These spread quickly from Italy to the rest of Europe. They were sung mainly by strolling singers called troubadours, who played instruments and sang in the streets in front of people's houses.

At first these songs were written in Latin. But by the fifteenth century, many of them were written in English. The first English carol that we know of was written at the beginning of the fifteenth century. It was a lullaby called "I Saw a Sweet, Seemly Sight."

Even though the early carols were lovely, they were not appreciated by everyone. When Oliver Cromwell ruled in England from 1649-1660, people weren't allowed to sing carols. Cromwell thought that Christmas should be a very solemn day so he banned carols and parties. Christmas was celebrated only by a sermon and a prayer service.

The British missed Christmas so much that they practiced it behind his back and the backs of some of the rulers who came after him. Finally, when Victoria became queen in 1837, people were enjoying Christmas music again. They especially liked listening to *waits*—musicians who were hired to perform in public. At Christmas, they strolled up and down streets, singing carols.

Many famous carols were written in the nineteenth century. "Silent Night," probably the best-known Christmas carol today, dates back to 1818. It was written by a priest who lived in Austria. His name was Joseph Mohr. On the day before Christmas, he was told that the church organ was broken and could not be repaired in time for the Christmas Eve service. Father Mohr was very sad. He adored music and couldn't bear the thought of celebrating Christmas without it. Suddenly, he got the idea to make up a carol that could be sung by the choir to guitar music. He sat down and wrote three stanzas. When he finished, he brought it to a teacher and organist named Franz Gruber. Mr. Gruber loved the words and wrote a tune to go with them. That night, the people in the little church heard the first performance of "Stille Nacht" or "Silent Night."

Another famous carol, "O Little Town of Bethlehem," was written in 1893 by a minister named Phillips Brooks. Before he became the Bishop of Massachusetts, he visited Jesus's birthplace in Bethlehem. He was so moved by what he saw that he wrote the words: "O little town of Bethlehem, how still we see thee lie . . ." He finished the song and gave it to Louis H. Redner, the organist at Holy Trinity Church in Philadelphia. Mr. Redner wrote the lovely tune that we know today.

The first American Christmas hymn was written before the nineteenth century. It was written in 1649 by a minister named John de Brebeur and is called "Jesus Is Born."

Some historians think the first American Christmas carols were sung by the Huron Indians. In the seventeenth century, a group of Hurons in Michigan who had become Christians gathered together during a snowstorm. They made a manger and stood around it, singing hymns in honor of the birth of Christ.

Just as the Hurons sang outdoors, people in Boston started singing outside in 1908. They walked up and down the streets, singing well-known carols. In 1909 another group in St. Louis

met and sang in front of every house that had a candle in the window. Today, groups of carol singers are found all over America. There are also Christmas concerts and special carol services that are performed on a large scale.

People of all ages enjoy singing carols. It is another Christmas custom that brings people together to celebrate a joyous occasion.

Christmas Cards

From December 1 until Christmas Day, people send cards to friends and relatives. The cards have lovely pictures of Christmas scenes on the front. They are often of Christ in the manger, the three Magi, a Christmas tree, Santa Claus, or stockings filled with gifts. Sending these cards is a good way for people to keep in touch with one another. They can scribble a message on the back, or enclose a snapshot of themselves or their family. The cards also make nice decorations. They are often strung together and hung, or placed face front on shelves and mantelpieces.

Sending cards is a new Christmas custom. It has been part of the Christmas celebration for only the past one hundred and fifty years. The custom of sending Christmas cards was started in England by British schoolboys. In the nineteenth century, they painted borders and wrote messages to their parents on sheets of paper. These were called Christmas pieces. Adults also sent gifts with messages, poems, and decorated notes attached to them. But this was not common. It was not until the second half of the nineteenth century that the Christmas card became popular. And no one knows who invented it.

The oldest known printed card is owned by Rust Craft Publishers in Dedham, Massachusetts. The card is made of paper lace and reads "A Merry Christmas to You" on the front. On the back, in fading script, is a message that says: "A Happy Christmas to My Mother Dear, 1839."

There is a card in the British Museum that dates back to 1842 (some people think the 2 looks like a 9, making the date 1849). On the card is a picture of a skating scene. It was painted by a sixteen-year-old boy named William May Egley.

Before these two cards were discovered, a man named Sir Henry Cole was credited with inventing the first Christmas card. In 1843 he hired an artist named J. C. Horsley to draw a picture of a family happily sipping wine. Next to the picture, he wrote "A Merry Christmas and a Happy New Year." Sir Henry Cole printed and sold a thousand of these cards.

When printing became cheaper and cards could be sent for only half a penny postage, thousands of them were sold in England.

The first cards reached America in the 1850s but didn't catch on until the 1870s. A printer in Roxbury, Massachusetts, named Louis Prang helped to make them popular. He started to print them in 1875. His early designs were simple, but they became fancier as time passed. He held contests and gave prizes for the best designs.

5 ❀ Christmas Eve

❀ ❀ ❀ Christmas Eve is perhaps the most exciting night of the year. It's the time when families finish decorating their tree and light the yule log. It's when children hang stockings and put out milk and cookies for Santa Claus. And it's the evening when the beautiful midnight service takes place at church.

Families often will wait until after dinner to decorate their tree. Then they can see how it looks when it's lit up in the dark for the first time. But there is no hard and fast rule. A tree can be decorated anytime before Christmas Day. Christmas Eve, however, is the time to light the yule log.

The yule log is an enormous piece of firewood. Sometimes it's the whole trunk of a tree. It's usually cut from oak, ash, or birch wood. Children in England like to cover it with mistletoe before it's carried inside and lit.

Like evergreens, the custom of burning the yule log dates back to before Christ was born. It was burned during the winter solstice to bring light and warmth to the darkest time of year. Its brightness was a reminder that spring would come again and crops would grow. Families hoped that the ghosts of their ancestors would come and get warm by its heat. They also hoped that its flames would scare away demons and bad spirits.

In ancient Scandinavia, the yule log was lit to honor Thor,

the god of thunder. Perhaps that is why Europeans believed it protected their homes from thunder and lightning. Until the middle of the nineteenth century, Germans let the yule log burn for only a short time. Then they took it out of the fireplace and stored it in a safe spot. Any time there was a thunderstorm during the next year, they put the yule log back on the fire. Supposedly, lightning would not strike a house in which a yule log burned.

People also thought the yule log helped animals give birth to more babies. The French soaked the log in water. Then they gave the water to their cows to drink. This was supposed to make the cows have more calves than usual. The French believed there would be as many lambs, calves, baby goats, and chickens as there were sparks in the yule log. When kept under the bed, the yule log was even thought to be a good cure for swollen glands and cold sores.

30

Today, most people don't have a fireplace that is big enough to hold a yule log. But when they light a small fire in their fireplace, they can think about the old yule log custom. Or they can find out if there is a local yule log ceremony. For example, there is a special yule log Christmas festival every year in Yosemite National Park in California. Four or five people dress up in white capes like the ancient Druids did. They gather together and carry a yule log, some holly, and a blazing torch indoors. They place the log in a great fireplace and light it with a piece from the previous year. If the log is still burning the next morning, the New Year will bring good luck. But if the log burns out, the New Year will not be a happy one.

Besides lighting a yule log, many people like to go to a midnight service at their local church. This is usually a much lovelier service than the one on Christmas morning. It is held at midnight because an old legend said that Christ was born at that hour. But no one knows for certain. The ancient Romans held mass when the cock crowed, which was about three o'clock in the morning. To this day, Spanish-speaking Americans call the midnight mass *Mise de Gallo,* "Mass of the cock."

During the service, the story of Christ's birth is read from the Bible. Often the church is lit up by candlelight to stand for the brightness Christ brought into the world. Everyone sings carols and hymns, and the sound of music fills the church with joy.

In the Middle Ages, the big bells in the churches in England were rung again and again between eleven o'clock and midnight. This was called the devil's funeral because of a legend that the devil died when Christ was born. As the clock struck twelve, the bells broke into peals of Christmas joy. Midnight chimes are still rung today to the tune of Christmas carols.

Christmas Eve is also when Santa Claus, the ancient gift giver, comes with presents after everyone has gone to bed. Children like to leave him a snack of cookies and milk so that he won't get hungry during his night journey. They also hang stockings from the mantelpiece or at the end of their beds for him to fill with gifts. According to stories that have been passed down through the years, Santa Claus leaves an apple in the toe for good luck and an orange in the heel if you've been good. In the olden days, oranges were rare and expensive, so getting an orange was a special treat. Santa Claus also leaves a nut for fun, some salt for good luck, and a piece of coal to keep you warm in the New Year. But mostly, he fills stockings with small toys and treats and good things to eat. The stockings add a happy note to Christmas as they hang, waiting for Santa Claus's surprises.

6 ❀ Santa Claus

❀ ❀ ❀ Santa Claus is probably America's most popular holiday figure. He has a white beard, a potbelly, and rosy cheeks. He dresses in a red and white suit and carries a sack of presents on his back. He lives in the North Pole, where he and his elf helpers make gifts all year round. Every Christmas Eve, he packs up his gifts and puts them in a sleigh. He hitches it to eight tiny reindeer. They pull him through the sky, and he lands on rooftops. Then he climbs down chimneys and leaves presents in stockings and under Christmas trees.

Clement Moore, the author of a poem called "A Visit from St. Nicholas," describes him as follows:

> *He was dressed all in fur, from his head to his foot,*
> *And his clothes were all tarnished with ashes and soot;*
> *A bundle of toys he had flung on his back,*
> *And he looked like a pedlar just opening his pack;*
>
> *His eyes, how they twinkled! His dimples, how merry!*
> *His cheeks were like roses, his nose like a cherry!*
> *His droll little mouth was drawn up like a bow,*
> *And the beard of his chin was as white as the snow.*

This Santa Claus story is really a combination of legends that have appeared for sixteen hundred years. They all go back to Asia Minor, where a famous bishop named Nicholas

lived in the fourth century. There are many stories about Nicholas's love for children. Once he brought three boys back to life who had been chopped up, salted, and stored in a barrel. Another time, he threw a bag of gold down a chimney for three unmarried girls who were very poor. (Perhaps this is why Santa Claus climbs down a chimney with his sack of gifts.) Nicholas was also famous for being able to stop storms at sea and prevent shipwrecks. He was loved by so many people that when he died, he was made a saint. He was called St. Nicholas and he watched over sailors, merchants, and children.

34

No one knows exactly how his good name spread from Asia to the rest of the world. Most people think it happened when some merchants in the eleventh century stole his bones and carried them to Bari, Italy. They built a large tomb and put St. Nicholas's bones on display. People from all over Europe could come and look at them. In those days, the bones of saints were considered very holy. Some people believed that they could even cause miracles. Men and women would travel for miles to see them. By the end of the Middle Ages, St. Nicholas was known everywhere. Four hundred churches were named after him in England alone.

His birthday was on December 6, and Christians celebrated it by holding a feast. They hoped that he would visit their homes on the night before. They thought that he'd come wearing the red and white robes and hat of a bishop and carrying a staff. They told children that if they behaved well, he'd leave them presents. But if they were naughty, he'd punish them. Sometimes, children were told he traveled with a scary figure who would carry out the punishment. One of these scary figures was called Klampus. Klampus looked like a shaggy monster. He had red eyes, horns, and a forked tongue. He dragged along chains behind him and rattled them when he was upset. Children were terrified of him.

Saint Nicholas's birthday is always celebrated in the Netherlands. Children leave out their wooden shoes on the eve of December 6, hoping that "Saint Nick" will fill them with sweets. They used to call him "Santa Niklaus," which became "Sinter Klass," which finally became "Santa Claus" when the

Dutch came to America. The Dutch settlers found it was easier to celebrate St. Nicholas Day in America on the same day as Christmas. That's why Santa Claus leaves presents on Christmas Eve instead of St. Nicholas Eve.

Santa Claus's home in the North Pole as well as his reindeer and elves probably date back to an old myth in Northern Europe. Thousands of years ago, people believed that the god Thor rode through the sky in a chariot pulled by reindeer. Snow and ice swirled around him as he stopped at houses for holiday dinners. The Northern Europeans also believed in elves or "tomtars" who had little beards and hid presents for children.

Sometimes, people get confused by seeing so many Santa Clauses at once. Some are standing on street corners, ringing bells and asking people to give money to the poor. Others are sitting in department stores, listening to children's wishes for presents. Still others are on television, telling about the many wonderful letters they've received from children asking for gifts. All of these Santa Clauses are jolly and kind, but they are only standing in the place of the real Santa Claus. The real Santa Claus is the Santa no one can see.

Americans look forward to the gifts Santa Claus leaves, but they also look forward to giving gifts of their own. As Santa Claus shows his love by leaving gifts, so people show their love by giving gifts to one another.

7 ❋ Christmas Around the World

❋ ❋ ❋ When people in California are waking up on Christmas morning, people in New York are sitting down for Christmas lunch. Meanwhile, in England, it's time for afternoon tea. In Russia, its suppertime, and the stars are beginning to twinkle.

Although people celebrate Christmas at different times all over the world, they share many of the same customs. Christmas decorations, music, church services, and gift giving are common to many nations. It's only some of the details of the celebrations that are different.

Germany

The German Christmas is very similar to our American one. The Christmas tree, some of our carols ("Away in a Manger"), and many of our recipes come from Germany. The German pastry, *spingerle,* or hard cookies with pictures stamped on them, is popular at holiday parties. So is the German Christmas tree pastry, *Christbaumgebäck.* This is a white dough that can be molded into shapes and baked for tree decorations. Germans also make beautiful gingerbread houses and cookies.

In parts of Germany, people believe that the Christ child

sends a messenger on Christmas Eve. He appears as an angel in a white robe and crown, bearing gifts. The angel is called *Christkind*. There is also a Christmas Eve figure called *Weihnachtsmann* or "Christmas Man." He looks like Santa Claus and also brings gifts.

Christmas Eve is special for another reason. At midnight, according to legend, cows are able to talk in honor of the cows who breathed on baby Jesus to keep him warm.

Besides these customs, Germans take Advent seriously. They hang up an Advent wreath with the four candles, lighting a candle on each Sunday before Christmas. They also have an Advent calendar, which has a "window" that can be opened on each day of Advent to show a Christmas scene beneath.

When Christmas arrives, the Germans like to give home-made gifts to one another. They are famous for their beautiful handicrafts. Before Christmas, there are special Christmas sales around the country where local artists and cooks show their work.

Sweden

Christmas in Sweden starts on December 13, or St. Lucia's Day.

Lucia was a young girl who lived in Sicily in the fourth century. She believed in Christ, which was against the law in Sicily. When a man who did not share her faith asked her to get married, she refused. The man was so angry that he told the governor, and the governor had her killed. Two hundred years later, she was made a saint.

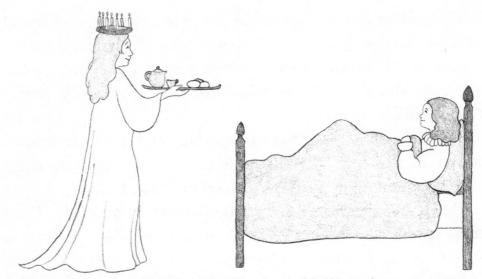

No one knows exactly why Lucia, a Sicilian, became popular in Sweden. Some say it's because she appeared to the Swedes in a vision one winter during a famine. She arrived in a glow of light, bringing food.

At dawn on December 13, the oldest daughter in each family dresses up as St. Lucia. She puts on a white robe and wears a crown of lighted candles. Then she wakes everyone, bringing them coffee, buns, and cookies.

Besides a St. Lucia in each home, there is a St. Lucia in each town. People vote on which girl will play the role. Once she is picked, she leads a parade of young people carrying lighted candles through the town. She spends all day helping the town celebrate.

The high point of the Swedish Christmas falls on Christmas Eve. After a delicious meal that lasts all afternoon, candles are lit on the Christmas tree. Then everyone waits for *Jultomtem*, a tiny gnome who comes in a sleigh drawn by a goat. When everyone is asleep, he leaves presents for people and extra food for animals.

Another gift-giving custom—*Julkapp*—is also popular. Someone knocks on the door, throws a present into the room, and runs away. The present is wrapped in many layers of paper. The longer it takes to unwrap it, the more successful the *Julkapp*.

Epiphany Eve arrives ten days later, and young boys dress up as the Magi and carry stars on long poles. They are called Star Boys, and they roam the streets singing carols.

Christmas is finally over on January 13—St. Knut's Day. An ancient ruler, King Knut IV, wanted the season to end twenty days after Christmas Day. People take down their trees, and children sing:

> *The twentieth day, King Knut did rule*
> *Would end the festival of Yule.*

England

Like Americans, the British enjoy beautiful holiday music. They also like to decorate Christmas trees and hang up evergreen branches. But they have some special customs of their own.

One of these is called mumming. In the Middle Ages, people called mummers put on masks and acted out Christmas plays. These plays are still performed in towns and villages.

The English also celebrate December 26 as a special day. They call it Boxing Day and give presents to mailmen, newsboys, and other public servants. The name comes from the old custom of putting money for the poor into boxes inside churches. On December 26, the priests would open the boxes and give the money away.

The English gift giver is called Father Christmas. He wears a long red or green robe and leaves presents in stockings on Christmas Eve. However, the gifts are not usually opened until the following afternoon.

Mexico

As mentioned in Chapter 2, Spanish-speaking Americans sometimes celebrate a *posadas* ceremony before Christmas.

In Mexico, the nine *posadas* days are the heart of the holiday celebration. On December 16 an empty manger is placed on an altar (*pesebra*) in each home. Friends and family gather together and act out the story of Mary and Joseph being turned away from the inn in Bethlehem. Then, on Christmas Eve, the altar is decorated with tinsel and flowers, and a baby Jesus figure is placed in the manger. Everyone celebrates his birth by singing, dancing, and feasting until Midnight Mass.

Also on each of the nine *posadas* days, there is a special children's game. After the Mary and Joseph play is over, each

child gets to whack a *piñata* that hangs from a rope. This is a paper figure that contains a jar filled with gifts, fruit, and candy. When the children whack it, it breaks, and the contents spill out. The young people scramble for their share of the gifts.

On Epiphany Eve, children put their shoes in the window. They hope that the Magi will pass by the window during the night and leave gifts.

Japan

Only 1 percent of the Japanese believe in Christ. Even so, most Japanese people decorate their stores and homes with evergreens during Christmas. The Japanese enjoy giving each other gifts, and this is the part of Christmas they celebrate. They have a priest called *Hoteiosha* who acts like Santa Claus. He brings presents to each house and leaves them for the children. Some think he has eyes in the back of his head, so children try to behave when they think he's nearby!

Italy

The Italians have a female Santa Claus called Lady *Befana* (the Italian word for "Epiphany"). She visits children on January 6 and leaves presents in their shoes if she thinks they've been good. If she thinks they've been bad, she leaves a piece of coal. Some parents tell their children that Befana will kidnap them if they don't behave.

There is an old story that when Christ was born, the Magi asked Befana to lead them to Bethlehem. She told them she

was too busy sweeping out her house to help them. She was
sorry later, and as a result, she is still roaming the earth,

looking for the baby. Like Santa Claus, she climbs down the chimney, but unlike Santa Claus, she arrives on a broomstick.

The Italians also set up a crèche or *precepio* in their homes and churches. They leave it empty until Christmas Day, when they add a baby (*bambino*) to stand for the Christ child. Families arrange the *precepio* under a *ceppo*—a wooden pyramid with shelves. Then they decorate the shelves with colored paper, cones, and candles. The *ceppo* is the Italian version of the Christmas tree.

On Christmas Eve the Italians enjoy a feast of noodles, pastries, and fish.

Russia

Before the Russian Revolution in 1917, Russians celebrated Christmas with great joy. They danced and sang from Christmas Eve until Epiphany. Like the British, they had mumming parades. They dressed up in costumes and traveled from house to house, accepting small gifts.

At first, Christmas was linked closely to their winter solstice festivals. The Russians used to sing songs in honor of the harvest god, *Klyad.* They hoped he would take care of their crops, and bring them a rich harvest in the spring.

Gradually, the holiday became focused on the birth of Christ. Instead of singing about the harvest, the Russians sang Christmas carols. On Christmas Eve, they strolled up and down streets, carrying "stars of Bethlehem" at the ends of sticks. They also went to a church service and shared a holiday meal at home. Special food was served, including a dessert of

45

steamed wheat, raisins, and honey, called *kutya*. On Christmas Day, the Russians ate a large meal, at which a suckling pig was sometimes roasted.

The Christmas season ended with Epiphany. Children loved Epiphany because on Epiphany Eve, *Babushka,* a female gift giver, left them presents.

After the Russian Revolution, the Soviets banned Christmas. Today, only the Russians who go to the Eastern Orthodox Church have a religious celebration.

The Russians who don't go to church have combined some of the Christmas customs from the rest of the world with those of New Year's Day. They decorate a New Year's tree and have a New Year's children's party. Children join hands and walk around the tree, singing songs. They dress up in costumes and wait for *Dyet Moroz* ("Grandfather Frost") and *Syyegorochka* ("The Snow Maiden") to bring them gifts.

Grandfather Frost is taller and thinner than the American Santa Claus. He dresses in red and white, blue and white, or white and white. He is not connected to St. Nicholas but rather to an old Russian folk hero. His helper, The Snow Maiden, looks like a fairy. She comes from a folktale about a childless couple who made a girl out of snow.

Africa

Because African Christians are spread out over the continent, Christmas is celebrated in many different ways.

In Ethiopia, Christians belong to the Coptic church. The Coptic church, like the Eastern Orthodox churches, follows the Gregorian calendar. Therefore, Christmas falls on Janu-

ary 7. Right before Christmas, thousands of Christians journey to the church in the city of Lalibela. On Christmas Day, a large group of nuns, priests, and monks form a line and climb to a nearby hilltop. There, they perform a special Christmas service. When it's over, everyone celebrates the rest of the day with dancing, sports, and feasting.

In Ghana, Christians have many of the same customs as Americans do. They send Christmas cards. Like the British, they have a Father Christmas, but he comes from the jungle, bearing gifts. They decorate their houses with beautiful flowers and palm branches. On Christmas Eve, children march up and down the streets, shouting *"Egbona hee, egbona hee! Egogo vo,"* meaning "Christ is coming! Christ is near!" Then they go to church with their families, where the candles on a giant evergreen or palm tree are lit. On Christmas Day, they give each other gifts, enjoy a large feast, and dance and sing.

Many foreign customs were brought to America by settlers. That's why the American Christmas is so special. It's really many Christmases rolled into one. It's a day when all Americans can share a common holiday.

If you know your family roots—or even if you don't—you and your family might enjoy visiting some ethnic holiday festivals. The ones listed below are based on the customs from "the old country."

Scottish Christmas Walk
  in Historic Alexandria
Contact:
YWCA
602 Cameron Street
Alexandria, Virginia 22314

Merrie Old England
  Christmas Celebration
Contact:
Boar's Head Inn
Ednam Forest
Charlottesville, Virginia 22903

Christmas Lighting Ceremony
Contact:
Chamber of Commerce
Leavenworth, Washington 98826

Christmas Around the World
Contact:
Seattle Chamber of Commerce
215 Columbia Street
Seattle, Washington 98104

Christmas in Old Salem
Contact:
Director of Information
Old Salem December, Inc.
Drawer F, Salem Station
Winston-Salem
North Carolina 27108

Christmas in Newport
Contact:
Bristol County Development
  Council, Inc.
154 North Main St.
Fall River, Massachusetts 02722

Holiday Fiesta
Contact:
Greater Myrtle Beach Chamber of
  Commerce
P.O. Box 1326
Myrtle Beach, South Carolina 29577

Yule Log Ceremony
Contact:
Public Affairs Administrator
Yosemite Park and Curry Co.
Yosemite National Park
California 95389

8 ❋ Christmas in the Kitchen

❋ ❋ ❋ Everyone looks forward to the delicious treats that are served during the Christmas season. It is a holiday of feasting with family and friends. It is the time of year when many people give parties and serve punch, eggnog, holiday breads, and sweets. Baked goods are popular Christmas gifts, too.

The main meal of the season is usually served in the middle of Christmas Day. Some families, however, prefer to feast on Christmas Eve. Italian-Americans, for example, often have a meatless meal in honor of the fast that was once held during Advent. Whether served on Christmas Eve or Christmas Day, the meal is lavish, sometimes with as many as twelve courses. A typical Christmas meal menu is roast turkey with oyster stuffing, cranberry sauce, mashed potatoes, creamed onions, and mincemeat pie.

To really have fun in the kitchen at Christmas, take out a book of Christmas recipes from your local library. Also, look through the Christmas issues of magazines such as *Family Circle, Ladies' Home Journal,* and *Good Housekeeping.* Try some of the recipes that are unique to other countries. Many of them, such as the recipe for German *spingerle* or *Christollen,* are difficult but are worth the effort. And, of course, you can always ask an adult to help.

The recipes that follow are a good starting-off point. All of them have been popular at Christmas parties.

Tips Before You Begin

1. Make sure you have the necessary ingredients and equipment.

2. Wear an apron. A lot of Christmas cooking is messy, since floury dough and greasy fingers are common in Christmas baking.

3. "Shortening" means softened margarine, softened butter, or vegetable oil. Butter provides the best flavor, but one kind of shortening can be used in place of another, unless the recipe calls for one kind only.

4. Flour: all-purpose, presifted flour is best.

5. If you do not have a sifter, place dry ingredients in a sieve over a bowl. Take a spoon and stir ingredients until they pass through the holes in the sieve to the bowl beneath.

6. It's easier to beat eggs with a fork or a whisk than with an eggbeater.

7. Instead of greasing a cookie sheet, try placing a strip of aluminum foil over its surface. This is a good way to keep the cookies from sticking to the bottom.

8. Preheat the oven for twenty minutes before baking.

9. Clean up the kitchen as you work.

Caution

Here are a few basic rules about safety:

1. Ask an adult's permission to use the kitchen before you begin.

2. Ask an adult to help when you:
    a) light the oven or burners.
    b) heat things on top of the stove.
    c) use an electric mixer or blender.

3. Turn the handles of hot pots and pans so that people will not bump into them.

4. Set hot pans down on a wooden surface, since some counter tops scorch easily. You can also use a pot holder or a trivet.

5. Use pot holders when handling anything hot.

❋ Cooking Equipment You Will Need

Nut chopper

Dry
measuring cup

Colander

Aluminum foil

Whisk

Rolling pin

Slotted
mixing spoon

Glass baking dish,
8 in. x 8 in. x 2 in.
(20 cm x 20 cm x 5 cm)

Cookie cutters in
Christmas shapes
(star,
bell,
stocking,
angel)

Large saucepan

Wire rack

Drinking glass

Mixing spoon

Sieve

Cookie sheet

Electric mixer

Bread loaf pan,
9 in. x 5 in. x 3 in.
(22.5 cm x 12.5 cm
x 7.5 cm)

Mixing bowls

Fork

Measuring spoons

Wax paper

Grater

Large wooden
cutting board

Eggbeater

Liquid
measuring cup

53

❋ Swiss Almond Drops

Ingredients:
3 eggs
¼ tsp. (1.25 ml) salt
1½ tsp. (7.5 ml) vanilla
1½ cups (360 ml) granulated sugar
1½ cups (360 ml) almonds, blanched and
    chopped
6 squares (6 oz. or 170 g) of semisweet
    chocolate

Equipment:
Nut chopper
Fork or whisk for beating eggs
Measuring spoons and cup
Slotted mixing spoon
Small mixing bowl
Large mixing bowl
Small amount of shortening to grease cookie
    sheet, or aluminum foil

What you do:
1. Preheat oven to 325° F. (165° C.).
2. Grease cookie sheet or cover with aluminum foil.
3. Chop almonds with nut chopper. Store in small bowl.

Chop chocolate squares and put into bowl with almonds.

4. Beat together eggs, salt, and vanilla in large mixing bowl.

5. Slowly add sugar, stirring constantly.

6. When mixture thickens and becomes the color of lemons, add chopped almonds and chocolate bits.

7. Mix well.

8. Drop by teaspoonfuls—1½ in. (3.8 cm) apart—onto cookie sheet.

9. Bake 20 minutes.

10. Let cool for 5 minutes before removing from cookie sheet. Makes 50 cookies.

❋ German Ginger Cookies

Ingredients:

1 cup (240 ml) shortening
½ cup (120 ml) granulated sugar
½ cup (120 ml) light brown sugar
⅓ cup (80 ml) molasses
⅔ cup (160 ml) light corn syrup
4½ cups (1 l + 80 ml) flour
1 tsp. (5 ml) baking soda
1 tsp. (5 ml) salt
1 tsp. (5 ml) ginger
1 tsp. (5 ml) cinnamon
½ tsp. (2.5 ml) ground cloves

Equipment:

Measuring spoons and cups

Mixing spoon

Small mixing bowl

Large mixing bowl

Sieve

Wax paper

Rolling pin

Large wooden cutting board

Drinking glass, 2 in. (5 cm) diameter

Small amount of shortening to grease cookie
    sheet, or aluminum foil

Cookie sheet

What you do:

1. Mix together in large bowl: shortening, granulated sugar, brown sugar, molasses, corn syrup.

2. Sift together in small bowl: flour, baking soda, salt, ginger, cinnamon, cloves.

3. Slowly add flour mixture to sugar mixture, stirring to blend. When it gets too stiff and floury to mix with the spoon, dump everything onto a large sheet of wax paper. Mix the ingredients with your hands. When it looks like dough (firm enough to shape), divide it and wrap it in two pieces of wax paper. Chill for two hours.

4. Preheat oven to 350° F. (177° C.).

5. Grease cookie sheet or cover with aluminum foil.

6. Unwrap one package of dough. Dip the rolling pin in flour and roll the dough out on a floured cutting board. If the dough sticks to the rolling pin, sprinkle it with more flour. If the dough sticks to your fingers, coat them with a tiny bit of shortening. Roll out the dough to ⅛ in. (3.18 mm) thick. (The thinner the dough, the crisper the cookies.)

7. Turn the drinking glass upside down, dip it in flour, and press it into the dough to make a circle. Pull away the dough around the edge of the glass with your fingers. Lift up the glass. Then pick up the circle left behind and place it on the cookie sheet. Repeat, rerolling the dough if necessary, until the cookie sheet is filled (about 12 cookies).

8. Bake 10 minutes.

9. Let cookies cool for 5 minutes before removing from cookie sheet.

10. When you finish with the first package of dough, repeat, using the second package.

11. Makes 50 cookies.

12. You can make icing for the cookies with the following mixture:

    ½ cup (120 ml) confectioner's sugar
    1 tsp. (5 ml) milk (add a few drops more
       to moisten mixture, if necessary)
    1 tsp. (5 ml) vanilla
    dash of salt

❋ Christmas Sugar Cookies

Ingredients:
⅔ cup (160 ml) shortening
¾ cup (180 ml) granulated sugar
1 egg
1 tsp. (5 ml) vanilla
2 cups (480 ml) flour
1½ tsp. (7.5 ml) baking powder
½ tsp. (2.5 ml) salt
4 tsp. (20 ml) milk
colored sugar crystals

Equipment:
Measuring spoons and cup
Mixing spoon
Large mixing bowl
Medium-sized mixing bowl
Sieve
Wax paper
Rolling pin
Large wooden cutting board
Cookie cutters
Small amount of shortening to grease cookie
    sheet, or aluminum foil
Cookie sheet

What you do:

1. Mix shortening and sugar together in large bowl.

2. Add egg and vanilla and mix some more.

3. Sift together in medium-sized bowl: flour, baking powder, and salt.

4. Add flour mixture to sugar mixture. Blend. It will be stiff. Add milk to make it easier to stir.

5. When it looks like dough (firm enough to shape), divide in half and wrap in two pieces of wax paper. Chill for two hours.

6. Preheat oven to 375° F. (191° C.).

7. Grease cookie sheet or cover with aluminum foil.

8. Unwrap one package of dough. Dip the rolling pin in flour and roll the dough out on a floured wooden cutting board. If the dough sticks to the rolling pin, sprinkle it with more flour. If the dough sticks to your fingers, coat them with a tiny bit of shortening. The dough should be rolled out to ⅛ in. (3.18 mm) thick. (The thinner the dough, the crisper the cookies.)

9. Dip cookie cutters in flour. Press them into dough, then drop shape onto cookie sheet. The cookie sheet should hold about 12 cookies.

10. Sprinkle cookies with colored sugar crystals.

11. Bake 8–9 minutes. The cookies should be removed from oven before they turn golden-brown.

12. Let cookies cool for 5 minutes before removing from cookie sheet.

13. When you finish with the first package of dough, repeat, using the second package.

14. Makes 50 cookies.

❋ Holiday Fruit Cake

Ingredients:
2 cups (480 ml) flour
1½ cups (360 ml) granulated sugar
1 tsp. (5 ml) baking soda
2 eggs
1 16-oz. (454 g) can fruit cocktail with juice
½ cup (120 ml) walnuts
¼ cup (60 ml) brown sugar

Equipment:
Measuring spoons and cup
Mixing spoon
Large mixing bowl
Small mixing bowl
Nut chopper
Small amount of shortening to grease dish
Baking dish, 8 in. x 8 in. x 2 in. (20 cm x 20 cm x 5 cm)
Plate

What you do:
1. Preheat oven to 325° F. (165° C.).
2. Grease dish.
3. Mix flour, sugar, and baking soda. Add eggs and fruit cocktail.

4. Pour into baking dish.

5. Chop nuts in nut chopper.

6. Mix nuts with brown sugar.

7. Sprinkle nut mixture over cake.

8. Bake 40–45 minutes.

9. Cool for 45 minutes.

10. Remove from baking dish to plate and frost with the following topping:

Mix together in small bowl:

¾ cup (180 ml) granulated sugar

½ cup (120 ml) shortening

½ cup (120 ml) evaporated milk

Pour onto cake while warm.

❊ English Walnut Bread

Ingredients:

1 cup (240 ml) walnuts, chopped

1 egg

1 cup (240 ml) granulated sugar

2 cups (480 ml) flour

1 cup (240 ml) milk

2 tsp. (10 ml) baking powder

2 tsp. (10 ml) cinnamon

½ tsp. (2.5 ml) salt

Equipment:
Measuring spoons and cups
Large mixing bowl
Small mixing bowl
Nut chopper
Small amount of shortening to grease pan
Loaf pan, 9 in. x 5 in. x 3 in. (22.5 cm x 12.5 cm
   x 7.5 cm)
Wire rack
Knife

What you do:
1. Preheat oven to 350° F. (177° C.).
2. Grease pan.
3. Chop nuts and set aside in small mixing bowl.
4. Mix together all other ingredients in the large bowl.
5. Add nuts. Mix some more.
6. Pour mixture into pan.
7. Bake 1 hour. It's done if a knife blade comes out clean when poked into the middle.
8. Let cool in pan for 10 minutes.
9. Turn pan upside down on wire rack. Let cool for another ½ hour. Remove from pan.

❋ Spiced Nuts

Ingredients:
¾ cup (180 ml) sugar
¾ tsp. (3.75 ml) salt
1 tsp. (5 ml) cinnamon
½ tsp. (2.5 ml) ground cloves
¼ tsp. (1.25 ml) nutmeg
¼ tsp. (1.25 ml) allspice
1 egg white
2 tbsp. (30 ml) water
1 cup (240 ml) walnuts
1 cup (240 ml) pecans
1 cup (240 ml) almonds

Equipment:
Measuring spoons and cup
Slotted mixing spoon
Large mixing bowl
Small mixing bowl
Fork
Colander
Small amount of shortening to grease cookie
   sheet, or aluminum foil
Cookie sheet
Storage container

What you do:

1. Preheat oven to 275° F. (135° C.).
2. Grease cookie sheet.
3. Mix together sugar, salt, and spices in large mixing bowl.
4. Separate egg white from yolk. Do this by cracking the egg on the edge of the small mixing bowl. Gently slide yolk back and forth between shell halves, letting white dribble into bowl beneath. Freeze egg yolk for later use.
5. Beat egg white with fork until foamy.
6. Add egg white and water to sugar mixture. Stir.
7. Add nuts, a few at a time. Stir until coated.
8. Remove coated nuts with slotted spoon and drain thoroughly in colander.
9. Place drained nuts on cookie sheet.
10. Bake 45 minutes, until golden and crusty.
11. Place in tightly sealed storage container when done.

❋ Eggnog

Ingredients:
12 large eggs
1 13-oz. (390 ml) can evaporated skim milk
1 cup (240 ml) confectioner's sugar
Nutmeg

Equipment:

Measuring cup

Large mixing bowl

Eggbeater or electric mixer

Mixing spoon

Sieve

Large jar with lid

What you do:

1. Beat the eggs together in large bowl until foamy.
2. Add milk and sugar. Stir.
3. Strain mixture through sieve and pour into jar.
4. Close lid and chill.
5. Sprinkle nutmeg on top when ready to serve.

❈ Hot Mulled Punch

Ingredients:

The peel of one lemon

1 qt. (950 ml) ginger ale

1 cup (240 ml) orange juice

1 qt. (950 ml) cranberry juice

2 cups (480 ml) granulated sugar

12 fat cloves

12 broken bits of whole cinnamon

Equipment:
Measuring cup
Grater
Wax paper
Large saucepan
Mixing spoon

What you do:
1. Grate the lemon peel by moving lemon back and forth across side of grater. Do over a piece of wax paper, so paper can catch gratings. Set aside.
2. Pour the ginger ale, orange juice, and cranberry juice into saucepan.
3. Heat over medium-low burner. It should simmer but not boil.
4. Add sugar, cloves, cinnamon bits, and lemon gratings. Stir until blended.
5. Serve hot.

9 ❀ Christmas Crafts

❀ ❀ ❀ Creating crafts projects is a wonderful way to help Christmas come alive. Homemade decorations add a special touch to every home. People also enjoy getting handmade gifts as presents.

The crafts in this chapter are things you can make for the house. You can find other ideas in magazines and crafts books in your local library. But, best of all, try using your imagination to dream up ideas of your own.

Crafts projects take up a lot of space. Before you begin, lay out plenty of newspaper on a large work surface. Put on some old clothes and an apron, since making things can get messy. Make sure you have all the equipment you need before you begin. You'll probably already have most of it, and the rest can be bought in a craft store or at the five-and-ten. Because there is some cutting and baking, ask an adult's permission before you begin. You might even need help on some of the projects.

Don't forget to clean up when you're finished. Have fun!

❋ Advent Wreath

Equipment:

Garden clippers
Outdoor greens, such as pine, cedar, fir,
    holly, laurel, or ivy
Clear acrylic spray
Scissors
Paper egg carton
4 tall candles
Styrofoam circle
    (from a craft store)
Pipe cleaners
Garbage bag wire ties
Red ribbons
Pine cones

What you do:

1. With an adult's help, clip some greens from outdoors. (You can also buy them from a florist.)

2. Spray the greens with acrylic spray so they won't shrivel later on. They should be sprayed outside since it's bad to inhale the fumes.

3. Tear out four egg cups from the egg carton. Trim the edges with the scissors so that they're even. Cut out holes on the bottoms, making sure they're the same diameter as the candles.

68

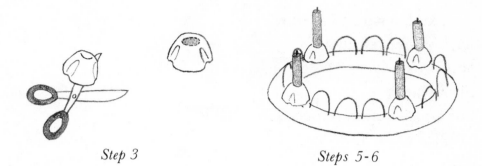

Step 3   *Steps 5-6*

4. Turn over the egg cups and insert the candles through the holes.

5. Stick candles, with their egg cup "collars," into Styrofoam circle. They should be evenly spaced. The bottoms of the egg cups should rest comfortably on the surface of the circle.

6. Stick both ends of each pipe cleaner into the circle, making a series of arches.

7. With the garbage bag ties, attach the greens to the pipe cleaners. Overlap the greens, so you can't see the ties or egg cups. Make sure the greens hang down over the Styrofoam circle.

8. Tie red ribbons to greens for decoration, add pine cones, and place wreath on table.

✿ Crèche

Equipment:

For barn:
Large cardboard box with flaps
Scissors

Craft knife or paring knife
Black poster paint
Paintbrush
Jar of water
Blue construction paper, 9 in. x 12 in.
  (22.86 cm x 30.48 cm)
Shiny gold star
Hay (craft store) *
Glue that is transparent
  when it dries (clear glue)
Ruler
Twigs

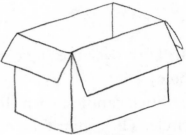

* Another way to make hay is to place grass on a cookie sheet and bake it for ½ hour at 350° F. (177° C.).

For figures:
Paper egg carton
Scissors
Poster paint, different colors
Paintbrush
Jar of water
Hay
Clear glue
Pencil
Straight pins, some with colored tops
Cotton balls
Piece of yarn, any color

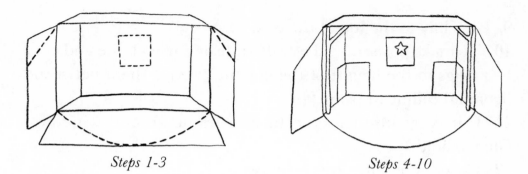

Steps 1-3   *Steps 4-10*

Felt and fabric scraps, different colors
Pipe cleaners
Construction paper—yellow, orange, brown, and white

What you do to make barn:

1. Lay the box on its side, so it opens toward you.

2. Fold out the bottom flap and trim its corners with the scissors to make a semicircle. Trim the tops of the side flaps at a slant, so that they slope downward.

3. Cut off the top flap. Cut it in two and set the halves aside.

4. With the craft knife or paring knife, cut a window in the center of the back of the box.

5. Paint the box black, both inside and out. Let dry. Store brush in jar of water.

6. Measure and cut a piece of blue construction paper to fit behind window. Glue to hold.

7. Paste the shiny gold star to blue paper, so it can be seen through window.

8. To make the backs of animal stalls, take the two flap halves from step 3 and fold them in half. Match the creases of the flaps to the rear corners of the stable, and glue to hold.

9. Glue hay to the top of the box.

10. To make posts, take the craft knife or paring knife and cut two twigs to the height of the box and wedge them between floor and ceiling at front.

11. Cut twigs into sticks to fit as a frame around window. Glue to hold.

12. Cover floor with straw and twigs.

What you do to make figures:

1. Tear out egg cups from egg carton.

2. To create manger, cut one egg cup across the middle to make two halves. Discard top half. Paint bottom half brown. Store brush in jar of water when you are done. Let paint dry. Fill with hay and place in crèche.

3. To make baby Jesus, wrap a piece of yarn around a cotton ball, leaving some cotton free for his face. Glue the ends of yarn to hold. Use two pins with colored tops for eyes. Cut a halo from a yellow felt scrap or piece of construction paper and glue to baby's head. Place baby in manger.

Step 2   *Step 3*

4. Trim the edges of the remaining egg cups with the scissors. Paint the cups blue for Mary; brown for Joseph, two shepherds, and a cow; white for two angels and a sheep; bright colors for the three Magi. Let dry. Rinse the brush under water, since you won't need it anymore.

5. To make people: attach head to body by sticking a pin through cotton ball to egg cup below. Add pins with colored tops to cotton balls for features. Cut robes and cloaks from fabric scraps and glue to bodies. Use yellow felt or yellow construction paper to make halos or crowns. Glue to hold. Use pipe cleaners for Joseph's and shepherds' crooks and glue them to their costumes. Place figures around manger.

6. To make cow: cut across the middle of remaining brown egg section. Discard top half. Bend two pipe cleaners double. Cut off the bottom halves. Glue bent middles inside egg cup at each end to form legs. Let dry. Attach cotton ball with straight pin to front of body for head. (Optional: Cut out ears and tail from brown construction paper and glue to hold.) Place in crèche.

Step 5　　　　　　　　　　　*Step 6*

7. To make sheep: repeat step 6, using remaining white egg cup.

❋ Paper Balloon Christmas Ornament

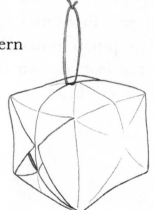

Materials:
Gift wrapping paper, any color or pattern
Scissors
Needle
Ruler
Cellophane tape
Clear thread

What you do:
1. Measure and cut a square of gift wrapping paper 8 in. x 8 in. (20 cm x 20 cm).
2. Fold corners A and D together to make a diagonal crease. Unfold and repeat for corners B and C.

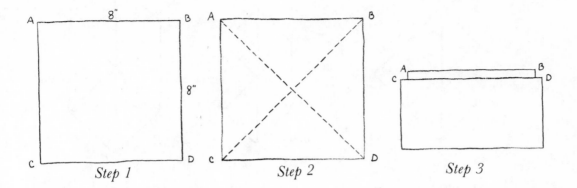

Step 1   *Step 2*   *Step 3*

3. With patterned side out, fold corners C and D to corners A and B. Now you have a rectangle.

4. With the index finger and thumb of one hand, pinch the rectangle at the center of the bottom fold.

5. With the index finger of your other hand, fold the lower righthand corner toward center between flaps. Repeat for lefthand corner. Now you have a double triangle.

6. Fold points A and B toward bottom tip E of triangle. Turn over and repeat for points C and D.

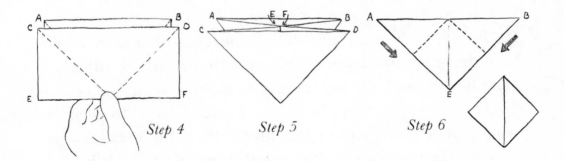

Step 4   *Step 5*   *Step 6*

Now you have a diamond.

7. Fold the top layer of side points F and G toward the middle.

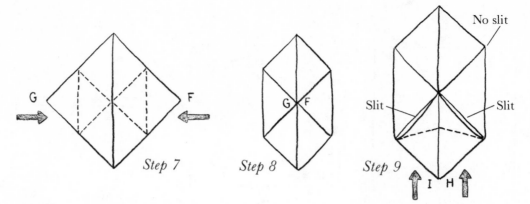

Step 7 *Step 8* *Step 9*

8. Turn over and repeat. Now you have a shape that looks like a hexagon.

9. Fold the bottom points H and I into bottom slits of side triangles. Turn over and repeat.

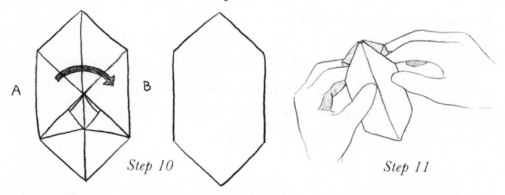

Step 10 *Step 11*

10. Fold sides A and B together. Repeat on other side. You'll have the same shape, but with a smooth, patterned surface.

11. Blow through the hole on top to make a paper balloon.

12. Cut a 9 in. (22.5 cm) length of thread. Thread the needle, tying a knot at the end of the thread. Push the needle down through the hole on top of the ornament. Then push it back up through the top, next to the hole, so that the knot secures the thread from inside. Cut the thread, leaving a 3 in. (7.5 cm) length for attaching to tree.

❃ Tin Tree Ornament

Equipment:
Piece of scrap paper
Pencil
TV dinner tray, throwaway aluminum pan,
    or aluminum from craft store
    (kitchen aluminum foil is too soft)
Hard rubber mat or magazine
Knitting needle
Scissors
Permanent felt-tip markers, different colors
Shellac or varnish with paintbrush,
    or clear nail polish
Clear plastic thread or piece of yarn

What you do:
1. Make a pattern by drawing a shape, such as a tree or circle or stocking, on scrap paper.
2. Place aluminum on rubber mat or magazine.
3. Lay paper pattern on top of aluminum.

Step 1
Step 2
Step 3

77

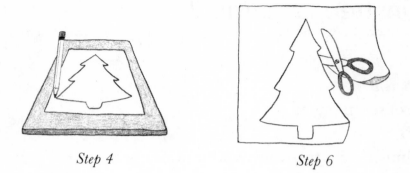

Step 4 *Step 6*

4. Trace around the pattern with the pencil so that the shape is transferred to the aluminum underneath.

5. Remove paper pattern.

6. Cut out ornament with scissors.

7. Color ornament with markers.

8. Use shellac, varnish, or clear nail polish to coat surface.

9. Make a hole at the top with the tip of the knitting needle. Cut a piece of yarn or thread 3 in. (7.5 cm) in length. Thread it through the hole and secure it with a knot. Leave other end loose for attaching to tree.

❋ Baked Tree Ornaments

Equipment:
Pencil
Piece of shirt board or thin cardboard
Scissors
Large bowl

Mixing spoon
3½ cups (840 ml) flour
1 cup (240 ml) water
1 cup (240 ml) salt
Aluminum foil
Cookie sheet
Rolling pin
Cutting board
Paring knife
Spatula
Sharp pencil or knitting needle
Poster paint, different colors
Paintbrush
Jar of water
Shellac or varnish with paintbrush, or clear
   nail polish
String or yarn, different colors

What you do:

1. Preheat oven to 350° F. (177° C.).

2. With the pencil, draw Christmas shapes on the cardboard. Cut them out and set aside.

3. Mix salt and water in bowl. Slowly add flour and mix to stiff dough. Knead dough in bowl with fingers. Add a few drops of water if dough is too flaky.

4. Place aluminum foil on cookie sheet.

5. With floured rolling pin, roll the dough onto floured cutting board. Place cardboard cutouts on dough. Use the paring knife to carve away dough around cutouts. (If cracks appear,

79

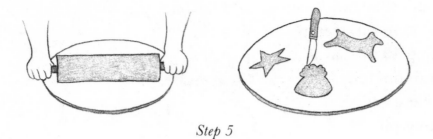

Step 5

apply drops of water to dough to smooth out the surface.) The shapes should be no more than ¼ in. (6.3 mm) thick. With spatula, remove to cookie sheet.

6. Make a hole at the top of each shape with the point of a pencil or the tip of a knitting needle.

7. Bake ½ hour. (Yield: approximately 20 shapes.)

8. Cool for ten minutes before removing to newspaper.

9. Paint the shapes with designs. Dip brush in jar of water to rinse out paint before switching colors. Let paint dry.

10. Coat with shellac, varnish, or clear nail polish. Let dry.

11. Thread yarn or colored string through holes to hang from tree.

❋ German Snowflake

Equipment:
Silver or gold wrapping paper
Ruler

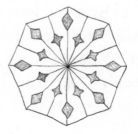

80

Stapler
Pencil
Scissors
Cellophane tape
Clear plastic thread or piece of yarn

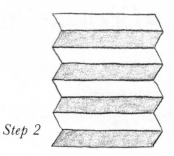

Step 2

What you do:

1. Cut out a piece of paper 4 in. x 9 in. (10 cm x 23 cm).
2. Fold into accordion pleats that are parallel with the short sides of the paper. Each pleat should be about ½ in. (1.2 cm) wide.
3. Stack pleats to make one thick strip. Bend strip in half to find center. Unbend, and staple together pleats at this center point.

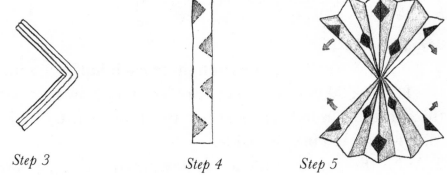

Step 3   *Step 4*   *Step 5*

4. Draw a zigzag pattern on the stacked strip. Cut out the shaded area as shown in drawing.
5. Carefully fan out the pleats on both sides of the staple to make a snowflake. Tape the edges where they meet.
6. Insert plastic thread or yarn through one of the holes. Knot to secure, and leave about 3 in. (7.5 cm) for hanging.

✸ Sponge Print Christmas Card

Equipment:
Red, green, or white construction paper,
   9 in. x 12 in. (23 cm x 30 cm)
Scrap paper
Scissors
Pencil
Kitchen sponge
Poster paint
Shallow dish
Rubber gloves
Felt-tip marking pens, one or more colors

What you do:
1. Fold construction paper in half, so each half is 4½ in. x 12 in. (11 cm x 30 cm). Cut along folded line. Now fold each of these sections in half, so you have two blank cards, 4½ in. x 6 in. (11 cm x 15 cm). Set aside.
2. With the pencil, draw a simple Christmas shape, smaller than the sponge, on the scrap paper. Cut it out.

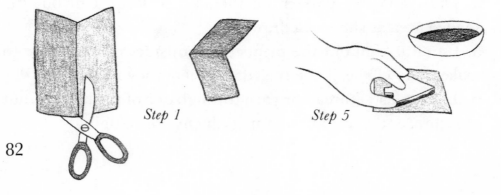

Step 1   *Step 5*

3. Place this paper pattern on top of the sponge. With the scissors, cut around the pattern.

4. Pour the poster paint into a shallow dish.

5. Put on rubber gloves, dip sponge shape into paint, and blot front of card.

6. When paint is dry, use the marking pens to add a Christmas message inside.

You can also make wrapping paper by blotting shelf paper with sponge designs.

❀ Candy Cane Ornaments

Twist red pipe cleaners around white ones to make candy cane stripes. Bend the ends to resemble a candy cane and hang from tree.

❀ Cranberry Strings

Thread a needle with clear plastic thread and tie a knot at the end of the thread. Sew the cranberries together. Tie a knot at the other end of the thread when you're finished, and hang string on tree. You can string popcorn together in the same way.

10 ❄ Christmas Games

❄ ❄ ❄One of the reasons everyone looks forward to Christmas is that it's a holiday from work and school. It's a time when people can forget their troubles and enjoy themselves. One way of doing this is by playing games. This custom goes back to the festival of Saturnalia. As mentioned in Chapter 1, masters and slaves switched roles. A slave-king was picked who made up games for everyone to play. In the Middle Ages, Blindman's Buff was very popular. As in mumming, the person who was "it" wore a mask. Today, families enjoy charades and electronic games. The great thing about games at Christmas is that they can be shared by people of all ages.

Charades

You need at least four people to play, but the more the merrier. Players are divided into two teams. One team goes out of the room. The players on this team choose a word of three or more syllables. Then they make a plan for silently acting out each syllable. The other team will try to guess the word. For example, if the first team chooses the word Saturnalia, they will have to act out the syllables SAT-UR-NAL-I-A. The person who acts out "sat" might keep sitting down until the other team figures out the first syllable.

When the first team has finished making its plan, it comes back into the room and performs in front of the other team.

No props are allowed. When the other team finally guesses the word, the teams switch. The team that guesses the most words in the least amount of time wins. There are other ways to play this game, but this is one of the best known.

Musical Chairs

Make a circle of chairs in which there is one less chair than the number of people playing. A volunteer stands by the stereo and puts on some Christmas music. Everyone else marches around the chairs. The person in charge of the music stops the music at will by lifting the needle off the record. When this happens, the players scramble for a seat. Whoever is left without a chair is "out" and takes away one of the chairs. This goes on, until there are only two players and one chair left. The person who gets the chair at the end is the winner.

Carry the Snowball

This is fun to play outside if there's snow. Otherwise, it works well indoors with cotton balls or apples. The players line up against a wall. Each player is given a spoon with a "snowball" on it. The point of the game is to be the first to reach the opposite wall (or North Pole) without dropping the "snowball." The game starts when someone yells, "On your mark, get set, go!" If a player drops a "snowball," he or she must start over again.

Hunt the Ring

The players thread a ring onto a long piece of string. Then they tie the ends of the string together. They stand in a circle, holding onto the string. The person picked to be "it" moves to the middle of the circle. The ring is passed along the string from player to player, covered by the players' hands as it is passed. When the person in the middle yells "stop," he or she has to guess who has the ring. If the guess is correct, the holder is the next person to be "it." If the person in the middle guesses wrong, he or she must take another turn.

Blindman's Buff

One player is chosen to be Blindman, and a handkerchief is tied over his or her eyes. The Blindman is turned around three or four times, then let loose. The object of the game is for the Blindman to catch a player and guess who the player is. Sometimes he does this by touching the other player's face. If the Blindman guesses correctly, the Blindman can go free. The person who has been caught becomes the next Blindman.

Maybe you can think up some games of your own or share the games you get as Christmas gifts. Whatever you play will only add to your and everyone else's Christmas fun.

❃ List of Suggested Reading

Barth, Edna. *Christmas Feast: Poems, Sayings, Greetings, and Wishes.* Boston: Clarion Books, Houghton Mifflin Co., 1979.

Barth, Edna. *Holly, Reindeer, & Colored Lights: The Story of the Christmas Symbols.* Boston: Clarion Books, Houghton Mifflin Co., 1971.

The Christmas Story from the Gospels of *Matthew* and *Luke.* Greenwich, Conn.: The Metropolitan Museum of Art, New York Graphic Society, 1966.

Del Re, Gerald and Del Re, Patricia. *Christmas Almanack.* New York: Doubleday Publishing Co., 1979.

De Paola, Tomie. *The Family Christmas Tree Book.* New York: Holiday House, 1980.

Dickens, Charles. *A Christmas Carol.* New York: Crown Publishers, 1980.

Menotti, Gian-Carlo. *Amahl and the Night Visitors.* New York: McGraw-Hill, 1962.

Meyer, Carolyn. *Christmas Crafts.* New York: Harper & Row Publishers, 1980.

Moore, Clement. *The Night Before Christmas*, illus. by Tomie de Paola. New York: Holiday House, 1980.

Pettit, Florence. *Christmas All Around the House.* New York: Harper & Row Publishers, 1976.

Purdy, Susan. *Christmas Gifts for You to Make.* New York: Franklin Watts, 1976.

Purdy, Susan. *Christmas Gifts Good Enough to Eat.* New York: Franklin Watts, 1981.

Shipman, Dorothy M. *Stardust and Holly: Poems & Songs of Christmas.* Great Neck, New York: Granger Book Co., 1976.

Thomas, Dylan. *A Child's Christmas in Wales.* Boston: David R. Godine Publisher, 1980.

Tichenor, Tom. *Christmas Tree Crafts.* New York: Harper & Row Publishers, 1975.

Index

Advent, 6-8, 39, 49, 68-69
African Christmas, 46-47

Bethlehem, 2, 3, 7, 25, 43
Boxing Day (December 26), 8, 41

Calendar, 7, 8
Candlemas (February 2), 7, 8
Candles, 6, 7, 15, 17, 19, 39
Christians, 3, 7, 12, 46, 47
Christkind (angel), 39
Christmas cards, 26-28, 82-83
Christmas carols, 13, 14, 22-26, 31, 32, 45
Christmas crafts, 67-83
Christmas Day (holiday), 2-3
Christmas decorations, 7, 9, 14, 15, 17, 18, 29, 67, 74-81, 83
Christmas Eve, 7, 8, 29-32, 39, 42, 45, 49
Christmas games, 84-86
Christmas Man (*Weihnachtsman*), 39
Christmas recipes, 50-66
Christmas tree, 15-19, 29, 41, 44; ornaments, 77-80
Cookies (recipes), 55-59
Coptic church, 46-47
Customs, 5, 27, 41, 46, 48

Druids, 10-11, 31

Eastern Orthodox church, 46
Eggnog (recipe), 64-65
England, 17, 31; Christmas in, 41-42
English walnut bread (recipe), 61-62
Epiphany, 7, 8, 45, 46; Eve, 8, 41, 42
Evergreens, 6, 9-10, 12, 13, 16

Father Christmas, 42, 47
Fruit cake (recipe), 60-61

German Christmas, 16-19, 22, 30, 38-39, 55
German ginger cookies (recipe), 55-57
Gifts and gift-giving, 4, 5, 39, 41, 42, 46
Grandfather Frost (*Dyet Moroz*), 46
Greek Orthodox church, 7, 8

Holly, 9, 10, 12-14
Huron Indians, 25

Italian Christmas, 43-45
Ivy, 9, 10, 12-14

Japanese Christmas, 43
Jesus Christ, 1, 2, 7, 13, 16, 31, 45

Kalends (pagan holiday), 5

Lady *Befana* (female gift-giver), 43 -45
Legends and myths, 10-16, 32-36, 39
Liberius, Pope, 3, 4
Luther, Martin, 15

Magi, 2, 7, 41, 43
Manger (créche), 21-22, 42, 44; making, 69-74
Mexican Christmas, 20, 42-43
Middle Ages, 16-20, 23, 31, 41, 84
Mistletoe, 9-12, 29
Mumming, 41, 45, 84

New Year, 5, 31, 46

Pagan origins and festivals, 3-5, 7, 10, 12
Plants, 9-20
Plays, 16, 17, 41
Poinsettias, 19-20
Posadas days (December 16-25), 7, 8, 42
Punch, Hot mulled (recipe), 65-66

Recipes, 50-66
Roman Empire, 3-7, 14, 23, 31
Rosemary, 14-15
Russian Christmas, 45-46
Russian Orthodox church, 7, 8

St. Francis of Assisi, 22, 23
St. Knut's Day (January 13), 8, 41
St. Lucia's Day (December 13), 8, 39, 40
St. Nicholas, 33-35
St. Nicholas Day (December 6), 8, 36
Santa Claus, 1, 29, 32-37, 43, 44
Saturnalia (pagan festival), 4-6, 84
Snow Maiden (*Syyegorochka*), 46
Spiced nuts (recipe), 63-64
Sugar cookies (recipe), 58-59
Swedish Christmas, 39-41
Swiss almond drops (recipe), 54-55

Walnut bread, English (recipe), 61-62
Winter solstice, 4-5, 29, 45
Wreaths, 6, 7, 9

Yule log, 1, 29-31, 48